Phau ntawv nyob muaj chaw:
(This book belongs to:)

_____

Npe
(Name)

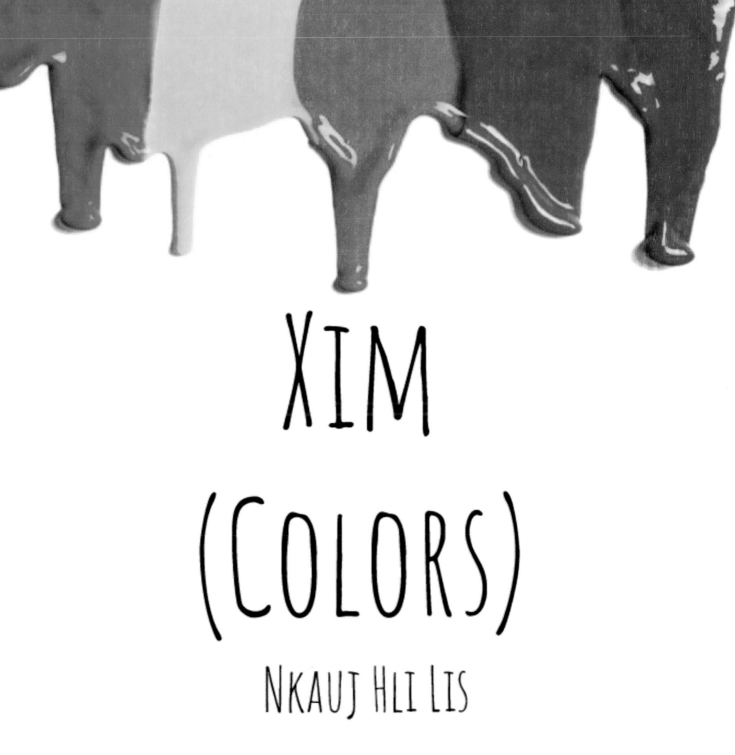

Xim
(Colors)

Nkauj Hli Lis

MY FIRST HMONG BOOK

DEDICATION

To my children, for having me recognize the
importance of the Hmong language and preserving
it for future generations.

Liab

Red

Kab ntxwv

Orange

Daj

Yellow

Ntsuab

Green

Xiav

Blue

Tag Lawm
(The End)

MY FIRST HMONG BOOK

www.myfirsthmongbook.com

Made in the USA
Las Vegas, NV
24 March 2023

69645520R00017

Liab doog

Purple

Paj yeeb

Pink

Tag Lawm
(The End)

www.myfirsthmongbook.com

69645523R00017